What I Want You to Know

What I Want

Tyndale House Publishers, Inc.
WHEATON, ILLINOIS

A Spiritual Journal to Share with Your Child

Douglas J. Rumford
Brian Roberts

Visit Tyndale's exciting Web site at www.tyndale.com

Copyright © 2000 by Douglas J. Rumford and Brian Roberts. All rights reserved.

Published in association with the literary agency of Alive Communications, Inc., 1465 Kelly Johnson Blvd., Suite 320, Colorado Springs, CO 80920.

Designed by Melinda Schumacher

Scripture quotations are taken from the Holy Bible, New International Version®. NIV®. Copyright © 1973, 1978, 1984 by International Bible Society. Used by permission of Zondervan Publishing House. All rights reserved.

ISBN 0-8423-3463-7

Printed in Singapore

06 05 04 03 02 01 00
 7   6   5   4   3   2   1

Presented to

By

Date

Dear

Love

Leave Your Children a Legacy

Have you ever found there were things you wanted to say to your children but couldn't because they were too young or it wasn't the right time or you were afraid you would sound mushy or silly? Have you ever struggled to find the words you wanted to say in the press of ordinary conversation? Have you hesitated to speak from your heart because communication has been cut off or you felt your children couldn't hear what you had to say at the time or you were just plain uncomfortable? The tragedy is that, unless they are written down, words of love are lost forever.

You will naturally pass on your genes, family looks, and material assets. But unless you do so intentionally, you may miss great opportunities to pass on your thoughts, values, and faith. We developed this journal to help you share your heart with your children—and pass down to future generations the most precious things you want them to know about you, your faith, your values, and your family heritage.

This book will be more than a diary of your child's first steps, first words, and first days of school. It will be a record of your memories, values, spiritual beliefs, and testimony of faith—a vehicle for preserving the treasures of your heart for future generations.

How to Get the Most from This Journal

What I Want You to Know is designed with a special introduction to journal writing and a three-tiered format intended to stimulate your thoughts in a number of areas. The three sections are:

My Story

This section is the place to record your personal and spiritual autobiography. The basic theme of the section is "This is what I want you to know about me."

Our Story

Chronicle memories of the life you've shared with your child so far in this section, which says, "This is what I want you to know about what it was like watching you grow up."

Your Story

This section is designed to capture your advice and counsel. It says to your child, "As you begin your life story, these are the things I most want you to know about life."

GETTING STARTED

Writing doesn't come naturally to most of us. And even for those of us who like to write, facing a blank page can be intimidating. So here are some pointers that should help you get beyond the obstacles to the joy of sharing your heart with your family.

First, just write! The very thought of other people reading this journal could make you freeze. But don't let the paralysis of perfectionism block your progress. You don't have to say things "just right." Simply express your thoughts and feelings. This journal is meant to be a living dialogue, not a sterile encyclopedia. Think of your entries as love notes, little letters to your child like the ones you may have slipped into a lunch bag. Start with the prompt on each page, but feel free to let your thoughts go wherever seems best to you. The stories don't have to be in chronological order. You may return to the same topic several times as new stories or ideas come to mind.

Celebrate the smudges. I (Doug) remember when my then-girlfriend (now wife), Sarah, used to write me letters, she would draw over any mistakes with swirls that looked like a caterpillar she called "Barney Bug." She would write next to it, "Barney Bug says hi!" As you write in ink, you will make mistakes. Welcome to the human family! We all make mistakes. But one of the most important lessons our children will learn from us is how to handle mistakes. If they learn to see them as a natural part of life, they will move a long way toward freedom. So be creative with your slips and smudges.

Beware of a preachy tone. Don't think you have to write your version of the Gettysburg Address! Be natural. Even the deepest things can be shared with warmth. You may have a concept of how you should sound on the written page, but that will most likely come off as artificial. Write like you would talk.

Be candid. It takes courage to get off the parental pedestal, but to be most meaningful, your writing must reveal your real self. Don't censor yourself. Honestly share your struggles. This journal will be most valuable if it truly reveals your heart. Your children will be better prepared for their own roles as adults and parents if they have your honest counsel and reflections to inform them. It would be better for your children to lift you up in gratitude, instead of looking up to you like a distant monument.

Give the reasons behind your responses. Share your heart, not just information. If you're telling your child about your favorite toy or book from childhood, explain why you loved it so much. Relate a story that explains what you mean. And where appropriate, tuck in an old photo or memento.

Date each entry. Dating is useful because you may want to return to an entry to make additional comments from time to time. It may take years to complete this journal! Also, the date of entries will often be of special interest to your loved ones.

Follow your heart. Keep in mind that the material we've provided to prompt your thinking is suggestive rather than exhaustive. Since this journal is so personal, you will want to adapt it to your own situation. As you get into the practice of writing, you will naturally express yourself on topics that come from your heart. Let the journal free you instead of restrict you.

Be ready for some surprises! As you write about a subject, memories may open up. You may find yourself laughing, sighing, or crying. That's OK. Be ready for the possibility that some topics will stir deep emotion, even pain. Don't let the feelings intimidate you.

Remember that it's never too late to start—or to start again! While you may want to start writing entries in this journal soon after your child is born or during early childhood, it's never too late to start. Even if your children are fully grown with their own families, you can still leave them a priceless inheritance that they can pass on to future generations. The time you take to write a sentence or two will be treasured for many years to come. Think of this journal as your spiritual will and testament.

When you give this journal to your child depends on you. You might consider writing more than one volume, with the idea of passing on the first volume when your child leaves home to begin life on his or her own, for college, career, or marriage. That way you'll be offering guidance at one of the most strategic times in life. Then you can begin another journal that you can write in indefinitely.

Other Uses for the Journal

Keep in mind that this journal is a tool for communication, for deepening your relationships with your children as they grow. You may want to use the prompts as discussion starters while on a "date" with your child. Move from the pages to personal conversation. When the journal brings stories to mind, you might want to tell them firsthand to your children or grandchildren. Consider putting the stories and memories on audiotape or videotape. Perhaps you could put together a video tour of your childhood neighborhood or a compilation of your family movies, photos, or videos. Be creative in showing your love. You will bestow a priceless inheritance on your family.

The prompts throughout the book can also be used as discussion starters for intergenerational groups, Bible studies, and retreats.

Story

THIS IS WHAT I WANT YOU TO KNOW ABOUT ME . . .

"WE PROCLAIM TO YOU WHAT WE HAVE SEEN AND HEARD, SO THAT YOU ALSO MAY HAVE FELLOWSHIP WITH US. AND OUR FELLOWSHIP IS WITH THE FATHER AND WITH HIS SON, JESUS CHRIST. WE WRITE THIS TO MAKE OUR JOY COMPLETE."

1 JOHN 1:3-4

My parents were . . . I AM 98 AS I PRINT THIS.

HARVEY HENRY HORN & FLORA MYWIFE
SISTERS, EDITH, PEARL & MYRTLE
ALL OF THE ABOVE HAVE GONE
TO HEAVEN ALSO. EDITH WAS 101
WHEN SHE DIED. HARVEY'S FATHER
FRANK CAME TO LIVE AT OUR HOUSE
WHEN MARION & I WERE FOUR YEARS
OLD.
FRANK WOULD SIT ON A PARK BENCH
IN FRONT OF LEONARD'S DRUG STORE
AND BUY ICE CREAM CONES FOR THE
NEIGHBOR KIDS IF THEY CAME BY.
GRANDPA FRANK DIED OF
WHEN I WAS 11.
GRANDMA FLORA HAD DIED WHE WE
WERE 3 YEARS OLD. WE HAD OUR FIRST
TRAIN RIDE GOING TO SOUTHERN
INDIANA FOR HIS FUNERAL.

WHEN I MENTION WE DID SOMETHING
ITS BECAUSE MARION AND I WERE
TWINS AND SHARED ALL OUR TIME.
MARION DIED SEVERAL YEARS AGO
IN NEW MEXICO.

GERTRUDE BEOHMER
HAD 12 SISTERS & BROTHERS.
BY THE TIME I CAME ALONG
THERE WERE 60. 2 BOYS DIED
ONE A BABY AND THE OTHER
IN ELEMENTARY SCHOOL.
ANTHONY WAS THE FIRST BABY
OF MARGARET AND JOSEPH.
KATHERINE, THERESA, GERTRUDE
EDWARD, HENRY, GEORGE, FRANCES,
WILLIAM, ANNA & DELIA. ALL OF
THEM ARE IN HEAVEN NOW.
GERTRUDE DIED OF ALHEIMERS.
SHE HAD BEEN LIVING WITH ME FOR
2 YRS AND I HAD TO PUT HER IN A
NURSING HOME. SHE WAS THERE
FOR ABOUT 24 MONTHS AND WAS 89.

What I remember most about growing up was . . .

What I know about our family "tree" is . . .

My childhood home(s) were...

WE WERE BORN ON JUNE 19, 1916 AT HOME. AUNT KATE WAS WITH MY MOTHER FOR THE BIRTH BECAUSE SHE WAS A PRACTICAL NURSE. I BELIEVE THE DOCTOR WAS DR. MORAN. I DON'T KNOW WHAT IT WAS BUT MARION WAS 5 MINUTES BEFORE ME.

MY PRINTING COULD BE BETTER BUT IT IS READABLE. I AM 98 YEARS OLD NOW.

School was . . .

The best advice I ever got was . . .

As I was growing up:

MY MOST EMBARRASSING MOMENT WAS . . .

MY FAVORITE JOKE WAS . . .

MY FAVORITE BOOK WAS . . .

My favorite song was . . .

My favorite movie was . . .

My favorite toy was . . .

My favorite television show was . . .

My favorite food was . . .

My favorite holiday was . . .

MY FAVORITE TEACHER WAS . . .

MY BEST FRIEND WAS . . .

MY IMAGINARY FRIEND WAS . . .

I had the hardest time in school with . . .

As a child, I was most afraid of . . .

I used to get in trouble for . . .

Some of the games I used to play were . . .

When I was young, I wanted to grow up to be . . .

My favorite family traditions were . . .

When our family went on vacations, we would . . .

My best Christmas present was . . .

My first [girl/boy] friend was . . .

My first job was . . .

The most influential person in my life was . . .

Here's how I met your [mom/dad] . . .

Here's how I proposed/was proposed to . . .

I wish I had tried to . . .

Jesus Christ became real for me when . . .

I felt closest to God when . . .

I felt farthest from God when . . .

I believe God called me to . . .

One of my greatest regrets is . . .

If I could live one day over it would be . . .

The most difficult time in my life was when . . .

I saw God work when . . .

I grew in my faith when . . .

I am happiest when . . .

For me, the perfect day is when . . .

I feel like my gifts are . . .

I doubted or had trouble trusting God when . . .

When I reach my final days . . .

Our

Story

THIS IS WHAT I WANT YOU TO KNOW ABOUT WHAT IT WAS LIKE WATCHING YOU GROW UP . . .

"I THANK MY GOD EVERY TIME I REMEMBER YOU."

PHILIPPIANS 1:3

We chose your name because . . .

My prayer for you at birth was . . .

When you were a baby, you would . . .

When you began to talk, you would say . . .

You made me feel special when . . .

I laughed so hard when you . . .

I was so proud of you when . . .

I was afraid when you . . .

I was so sad when you . . .

Some of my favorite times with you have been . . .

I'll never forget watching you when . . .

It hurt to see you struggle with . . .

You drove me crazy when you . . .

I saw God work in your life when . . .

I hope you will always . . .

The hardest thing for me as a parent was (is)...

My favorite things about you are . . .

When I think about your leaving, I feel . . .

To me, one of the most important things you ever did was . . .

You have a gift for . . .

Your

Story

As you enter a new phase of your story, these are the things I most want you to know about life . . .

"Be diligent in these matters; give yourself wholly to them, so that everyone may see your progress. Watch your life and doctrine closely. Persevere in them, because if you do, you will save both yourself and your hearers."

1 Timothy 4:15-16

My hope for you is . . .

As you graduate . . .

My philosophy toward work has always been . . .

When you are looking for friends . . .

Money means . . .

A woman is . . .

A man is . . .

The most important qualities to look for in a spouse are . . .

You will find joy . . .

When you fail . . .

When you succeed . . .

When you are tempted . . .

When you are afraid . . .

When you worry . . .

When you doubt . . .

When you get angry . . .

When others don't meet your expectations . . .

When you are depressed . . .

When you are sick . . .

When you feel like giving up . . .

When you are trying to determine God's will . . .

When you have to make an important decision . . .

When you are looking for security . . .

If I could give you one gift, it would be . . .

I have found that being a parent means . . .

When you have your first child . . .

If you don't have children . . .

When you suffer loss . . .

When you feel betrayed . . .

I hope you will remember me as . . .

When you face grief . . .

When you feel you have let God down . . .

When you feel God has let you down . . .

Faith means . . .

My favorite Bible passages are . . . because . . .

I believe death is . . .

I bless you with . . .